To Melissa
with our love
from
Grandpa + Granny
Christmas 1984

THE GOORI GOORI BIRD

From a Legend of the Bidjara People
of the Upper Warrego

Grahame L. Walsh
Illustrated by John Morrison

University of Queensland Press

First published 1984 by University of Queensland Press
Box 42, St Lucia, Queensland, Australia

© Grahame Walsh and John Morrison 1984

This book is copyright. Apart from any fair dealing for the
purposes of private study, research, criticism or review, as
permitted under the Copyright Act, no part may be reproduced
by any process without written permission. Enquiries should
be made to the publisher.

Typeset by Savage Type Pty Ltd
Printed in Korea by Pyung Hwa Dang Printing Co. Ltd.

Distributed in the UK, Europe, the Middle East, Africa, and the
Caribbean by Prentice Hall International, International Book
Distributors Ltd, 66 Wood Lane End, Hemel Hempstead, Herts.,
England

Distributed in the USA and Canada by Technical Impex
Corporation, 5 South Union Street, Lawrence, Mass. 01843 USA

Cataloguing in Publication Data

National Library of Australia

Walsh, Grahame, 1945-
   The goori goori bird.

   For children.

   [1]. Aborigines, Australian — Legends —
Juvenile literature. 2. Legends — Australia —
Juvenile literature. I. Morrison, John.
II. Title.

398.2'049915

ISBN 0 7022 1777 8.

Preserving Central Queensland Rock Art

The wealth of rock art found in the ranges surrounding Carnarvon Gorge in central Queensland represents the culture of a race that lived here for more than 19,000 years. The art is an irreplaceable part of our heritage.

   The national parks of central Queensland contain examples of Australia's natural environment and its outstanding scenery. They also include many rock art sites. The sites are an important part of these park values. They are tangible links in appreciating our relationships with the environment. Tales such as *The Goori Goori Bird* add a further dimension to our understanding. The telling of the story complements the work the National Parks and Wildlife Service has been doing in managing and protecting rock art sites in central Queensland. At Carnarvon Gorge you may visit art sites where boardwalks and information are provided to help you appreciate and learn without damaging the art.

   Proceeds the author may receive from the sale of this book will be directed into a trust to be used only for the preservation of the rapidly vanishing Aboriginal rock art in this area. Financial support will be offered to worthwhile projects unable to gain support from other sources.

   Enjoy this story and appreciate the art.

 QUEENSLAND NATIONAL PARKS AND WILDLIFE SERVICE

Dr G.W. Saunders
Director
National Parks and Wildlife Service

Gone but not forgotten, may the children of the Dreamtime live on forever in the spirit of Carnarvon.

Back in the Dreamtime there lived a huge "devil bird" of frightening appearance. He looked like Gooridithalla the wedgetail eagle, only much larger, and he lived on flesh. He was called the Goori Goori bird.

The Goori Goori bird had built a nest at the top of the highest tree in a remote Maigal forest at the crest of the Great Dividing Range. This was in the Bidjara people's tribal territory, which was the headwaters of Budhurradala, the Warrego River.

Few people had visited this remote tableland, and none had seen the bird's nest, which was so high that it was often hidden by clouds.

Soon the animals became wary, and the huge bird was unable to kill enough to satisfy his hunger. He then began preying on Aboriginal children who had foolishly become lost or separated from their parents.

From his lofty position, soaring over the rugged gorges, he would swoop down beside a lost child.

Speaking in his most pleasant voice, saying he was a friend, he would then get the child to climb onto his back so that he could fly him out in search of his parents. Once on the bird's back, the child would be flown to the hidden nest and eaten by the evil Goori Goori bird.

So many children disappeared without trace that the old men of the tribe decided that an evil spirit, or Yakajah, must be causing the trouble.

Forgetting the warnings, one little boy called Wangurd wandered away from his mother, searching for ripe berries on the Doonbulga bushes. He was always hungry, and that is why he had been given the name Wangurd, which means "big eater".

Running from bush to bush, he gobbled as many of the sweet berries as he could pick, and soon became quite lost. When he could eat no more, he began looking for his mother, but the more he searched the more he became lost.

Silently soaring high above, the Goori Goori bird had been watching the careless child, and swiftly swooped down to land softly beside him. His frightening appearance scared Wangurd, but his friendly voice and kind offers of help soon made the boy forget his fears.

Although Wangurd did not want to climb on the bird's back, he was too afraid to stay there alone with the sun already low.

With Wangurd clinging to his neck, the Goori Goori bird flew off. The clever boy quickly realized that he was flying high up the gorges to the range, to an area which his family never went near. Realizing he was being tricked and that he was in danger, Wangurd knew he must escape from the bird before they reached his hideaway.

Thinking quickly, Wangurd pretended to be afraid of the height at which they were flying, calling to the bird to fly lower. Repeating the plea several times, Wangurd soon had the bird flying just above the rocky cliff tops.

While flying over a patch of sand, Wangurd slipped from the bird's back, jumped to the soft ground, and quickly hid himself.

The giant bird did not feel the small boy roll off his back, and continued flying to his nest. When he landed and found that the clever boy had tricked him, he became very angry.

Wangurd had watched the bird fly into the towering Maigal forest, and knew that the nest must be up there hidden in the clouds.

Just as the sun was setting, Wangurd heard his father's voice calling in the distance, and soon the lucky boy was back with the tribe.

That night Wangurd told the tribe of his flight with the Goori Goori bird, and how he had tricked him. The tribal elders decided this evil bird that had taken so many children must be killed quickly.

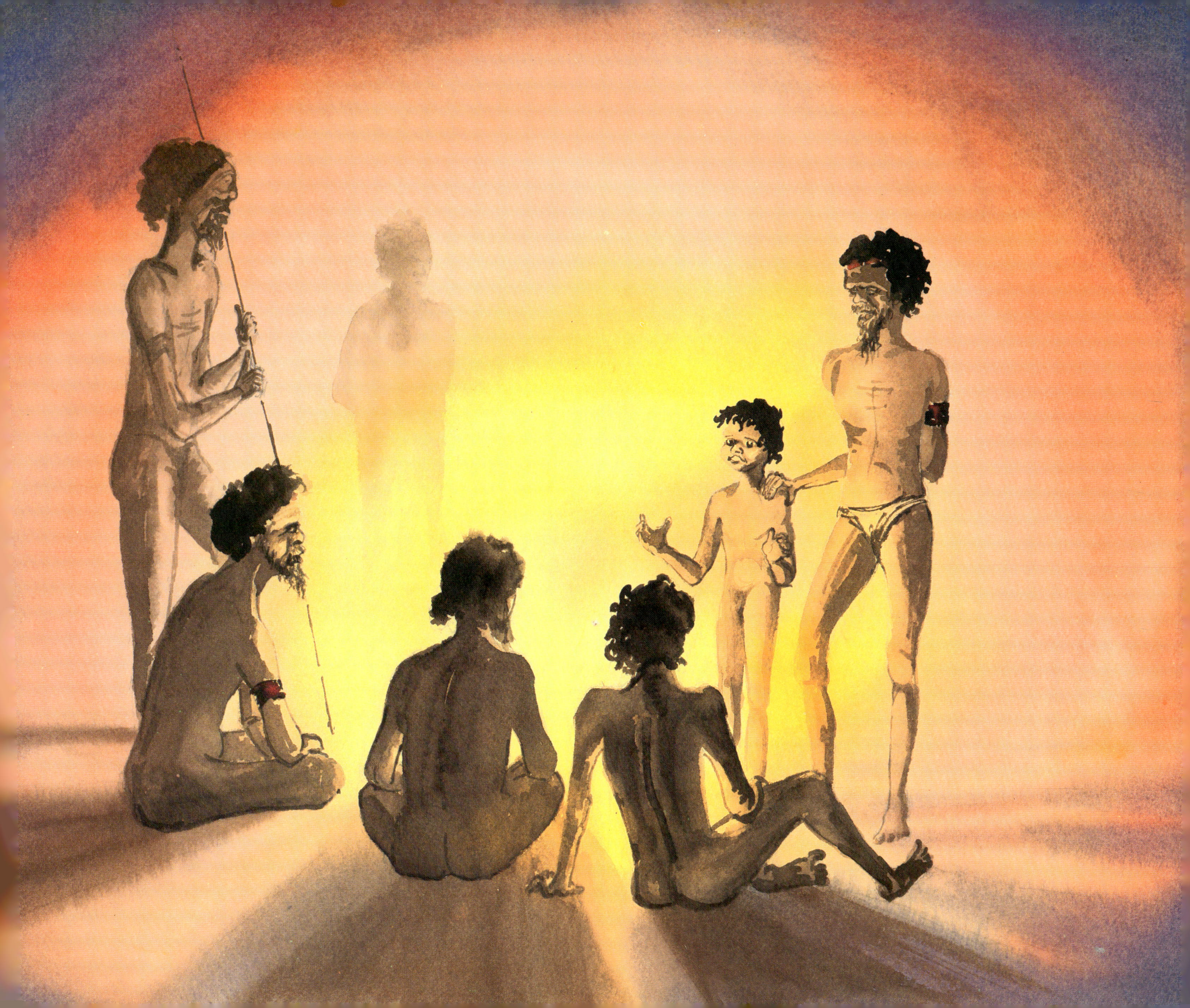

Next day Wangurd went with his father and another warrior on the long trip to the Maigal forest, searching for the bird's hideout. Hearing the loud snores of the sleeping bird, the sound led them to the tallest tree, where they saw the nest.

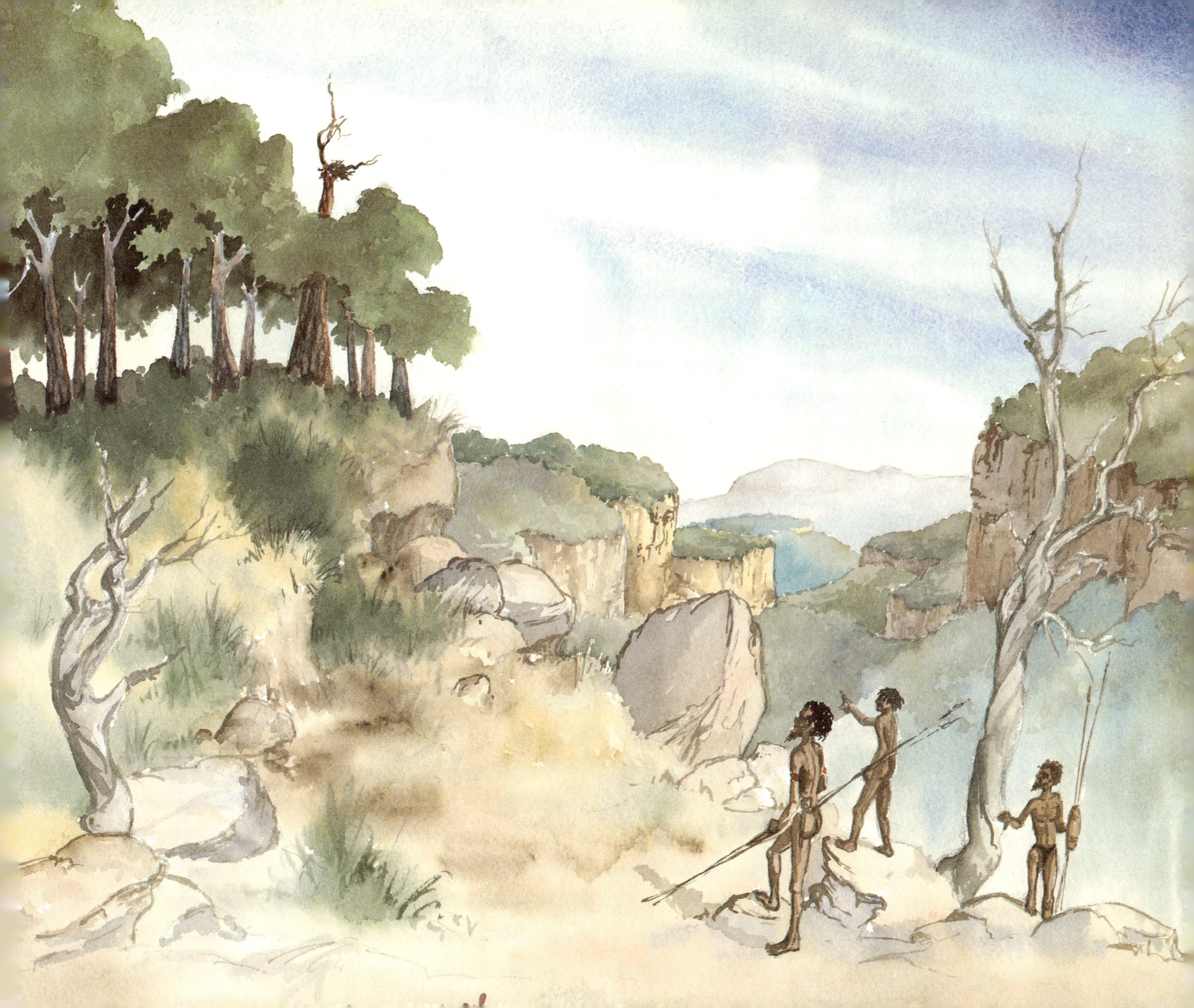

Hiding, they waited till the bird awoke and flew off in search of food.

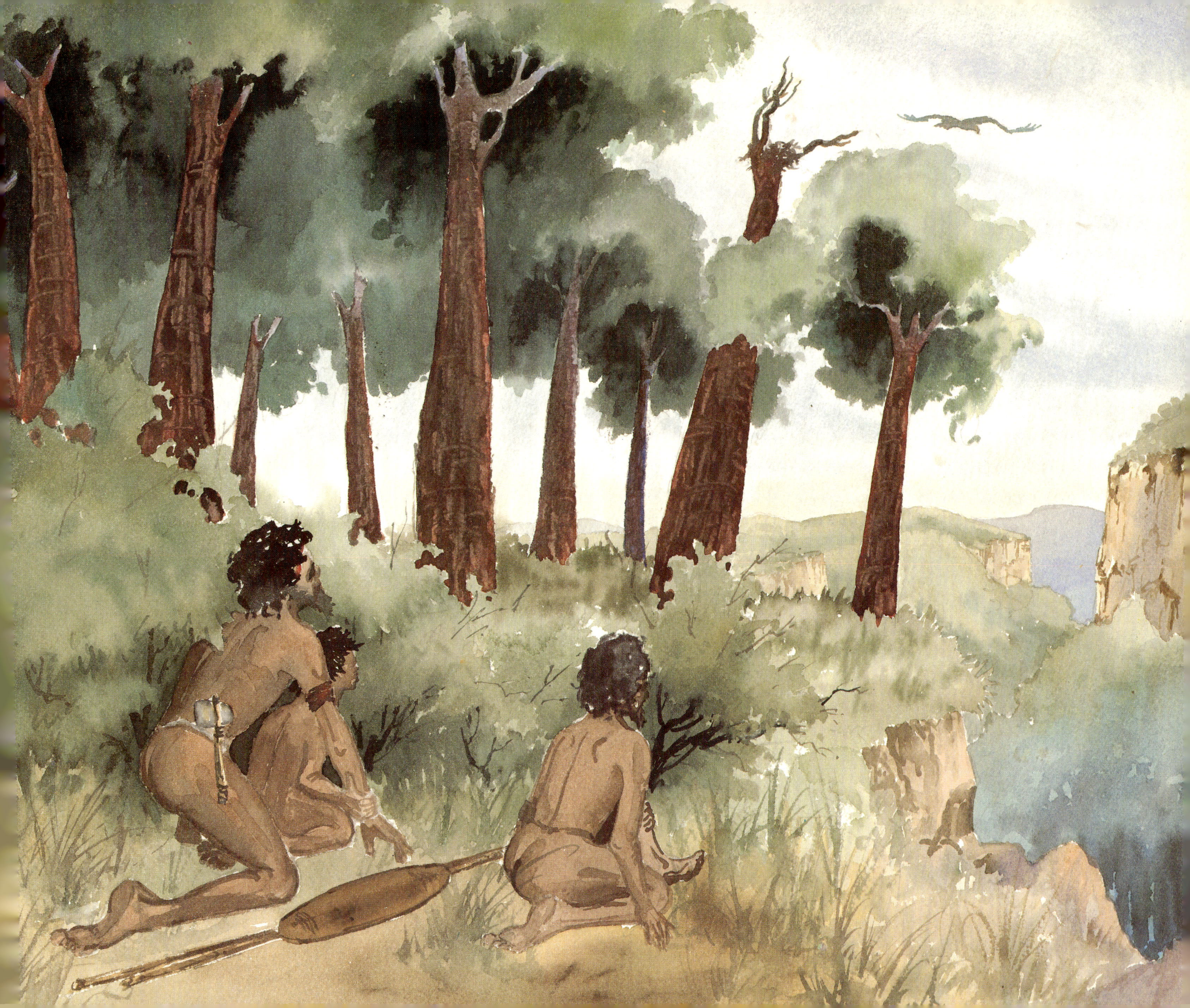

Taking their stone tomahawks, the men cut climbing toe-holds up the tree trunk to the nest, then returned to their hide to await the bird's arrival.

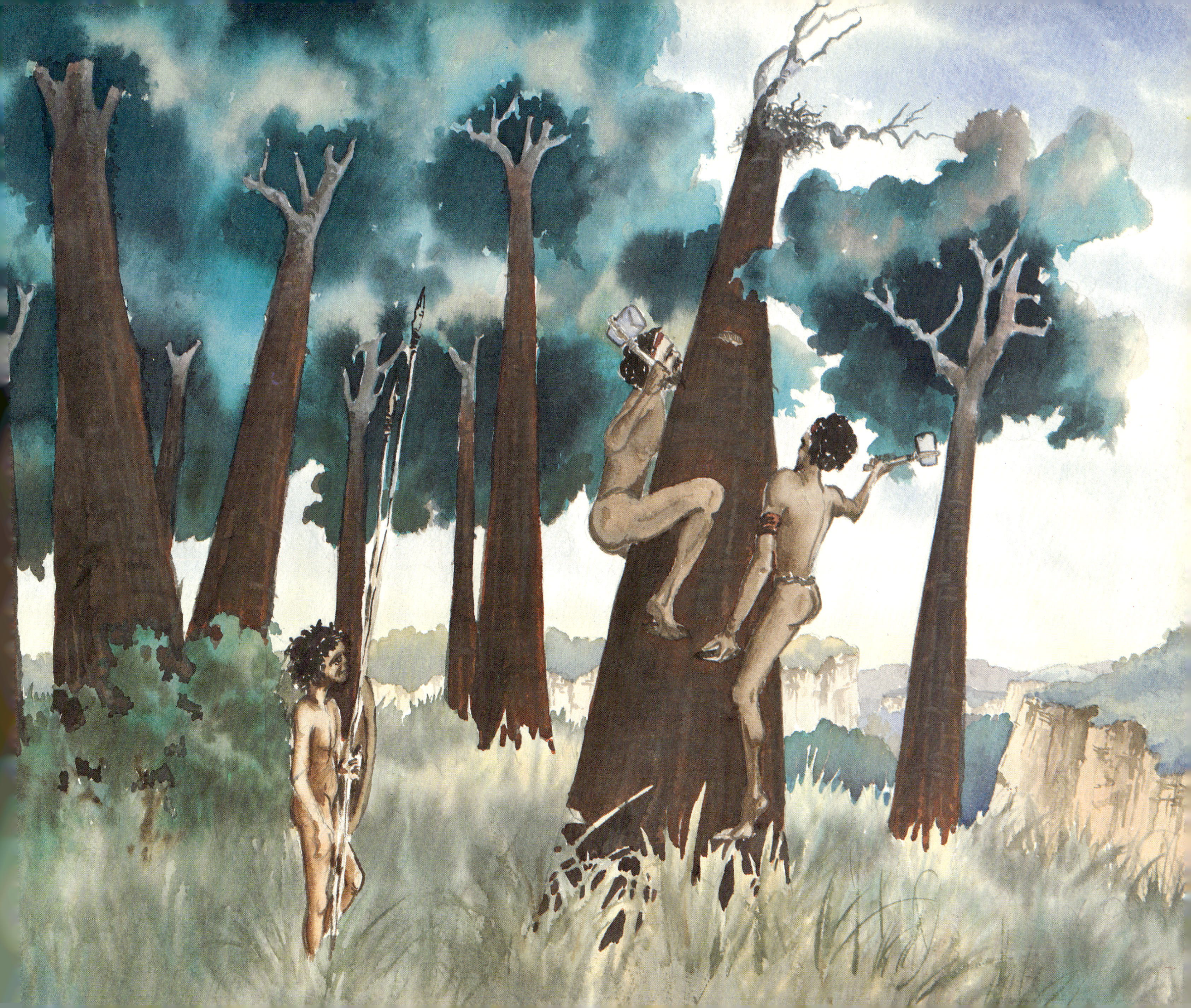

Late in the evening the bird returned to the nest, soon falling asleep and snoring loudly. Wangurd's father quickly got a small fire burning, and lit two big firesticks. Carrying the burning firesticks, the two warriors climbed the tree trunk and soon had the underside of the nest blazing.

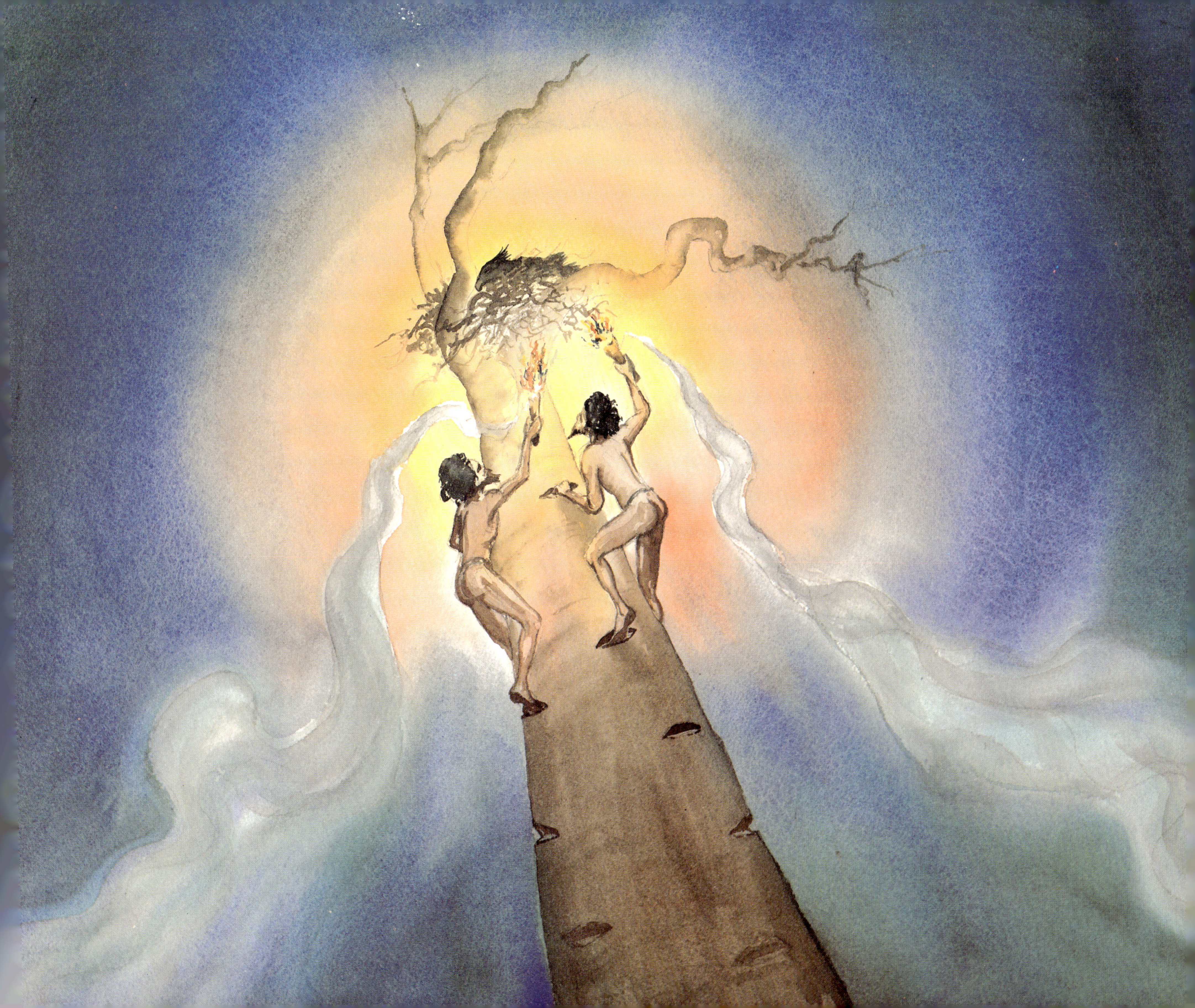

From their hide in the bushes, Wangurd and the warriors watched the roaring fire which soon burnt through the sleeping bird's nest, setting fire to one of his legs.

Awakening with a cry of pain, the Goori Goori bird leapt from his blazing nest, flying westwards across the night sky. As he desperately searched for water to put out the fire on his leg, he left a trail of sparks and burning feathers.

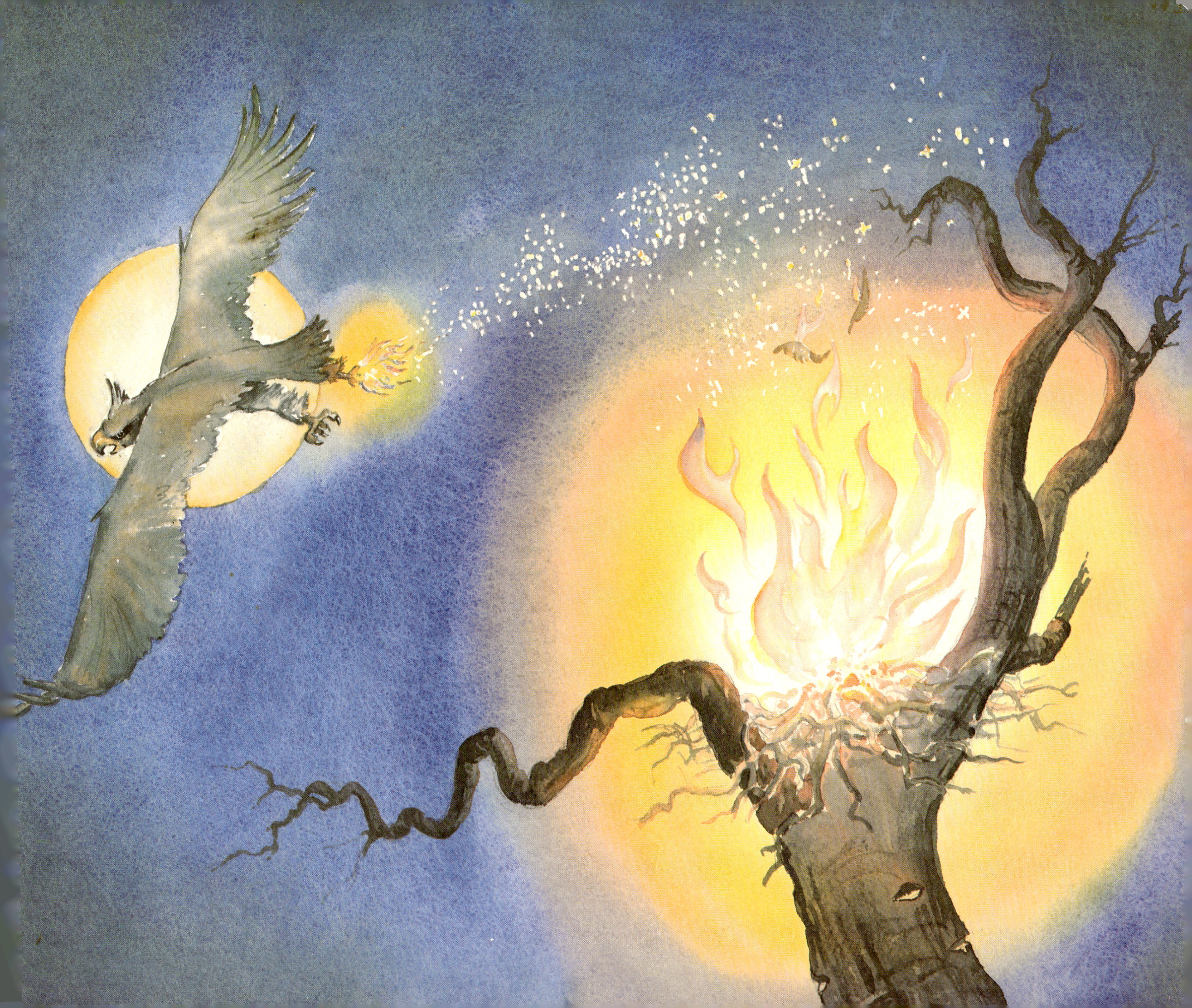

Flying a long way to the west, he saw a big lake, and flopped down into it, sitting with his one good leg in the mud, and the burnt off stump of the other in the water. The crippled bird never again returned to the gorges of the ranges, and the Bidjara children were once again safe.

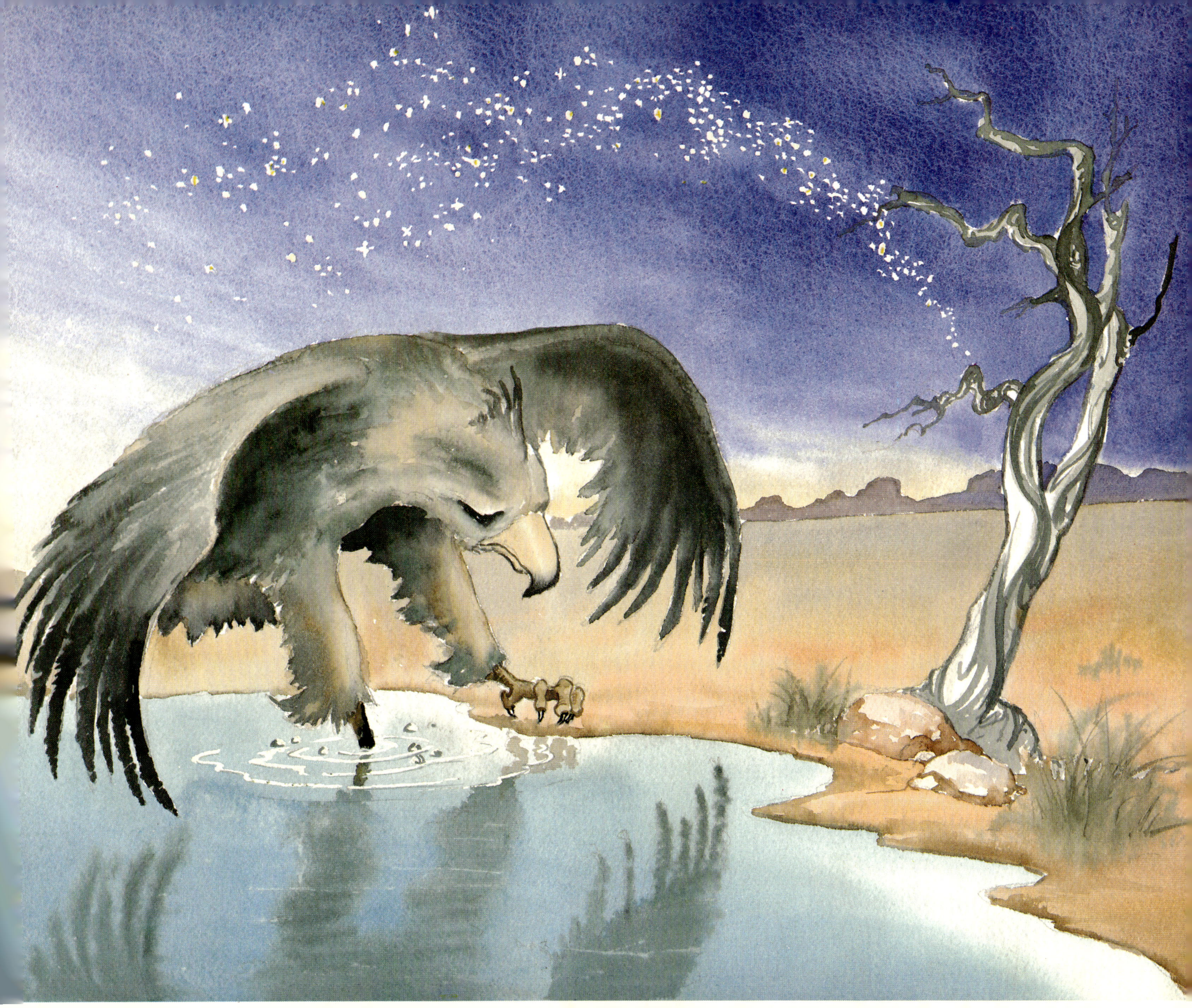

The great arch of sparks and burning feathers left by the Goori Goori bird as he flew from Budhurradala to the western lake remained in the sky, and became Budhanbil, the Milky Way.

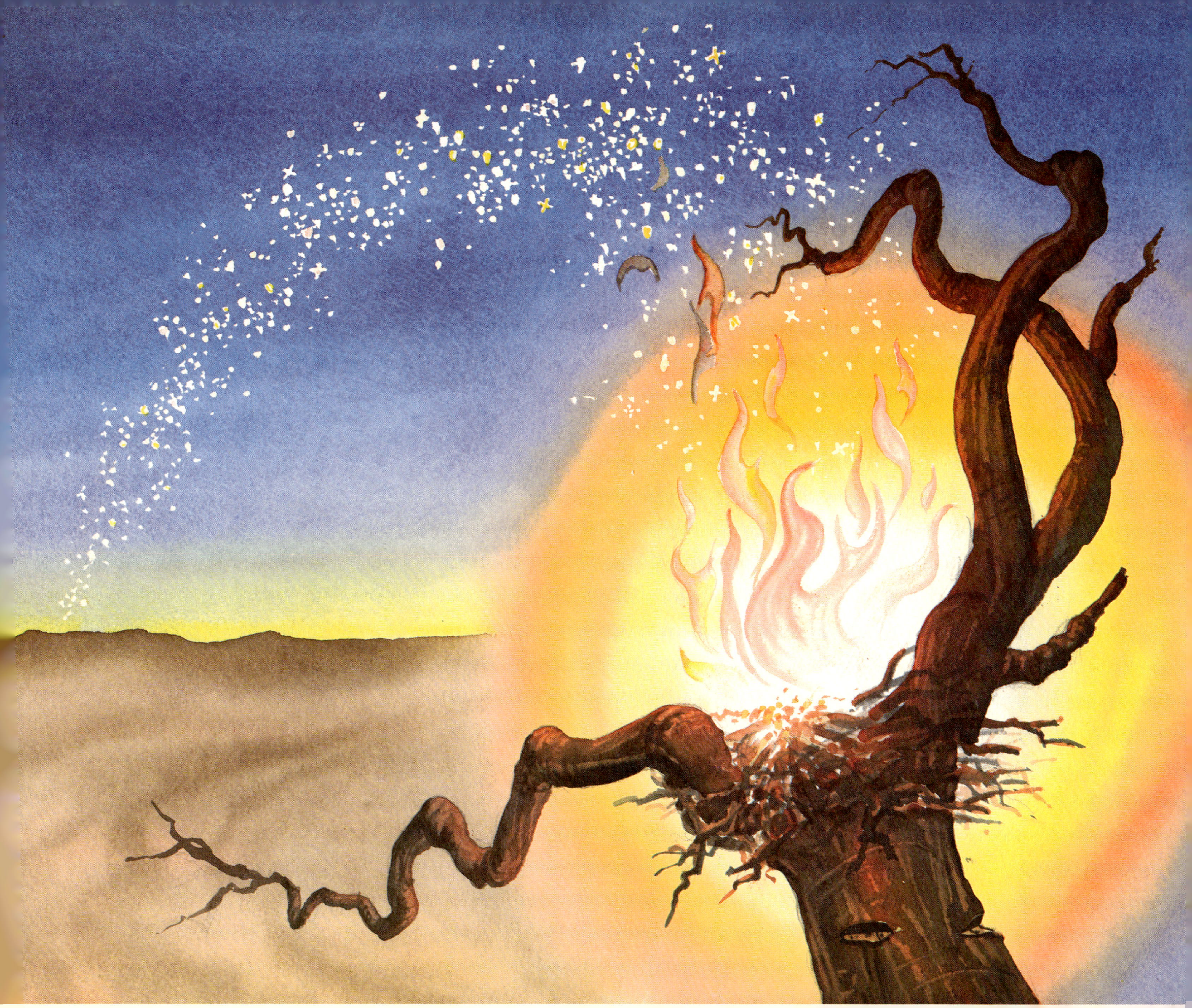

Wangurd and the warriors were treated as heroes when they returned to their tribe. They celebrated with a new dance showing how Budhanbil the Milky Way was formed and the dance became a favourite performance at corroborees from that day on.

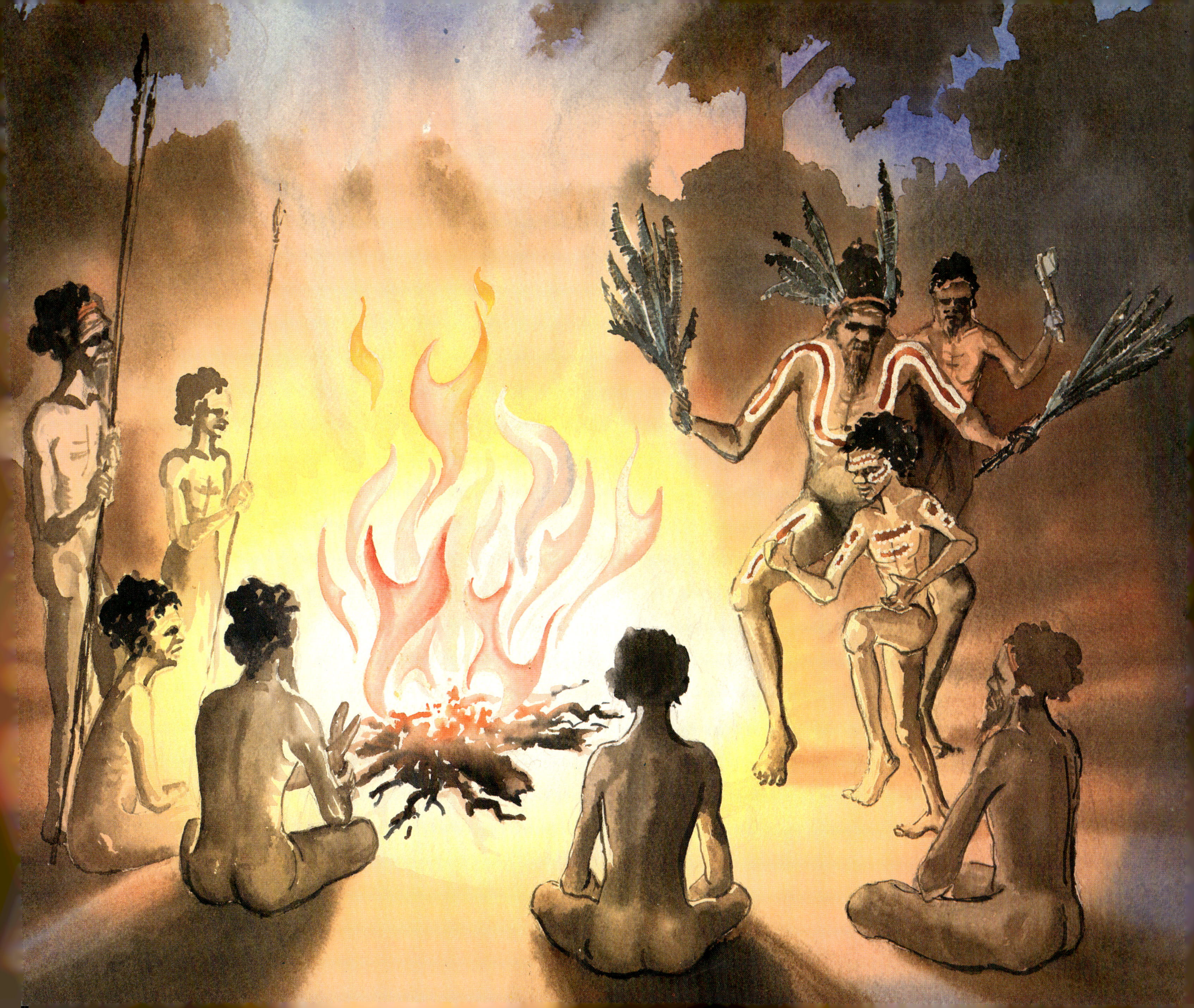

Grahame Walsh (author)

Born at Roma in Central Queensland, Grahame was raised on his parents' sheep and cattle station near Injune, on the southern fall of the Carnarvon Ranges.

His deep interest in the local Aboriginal prehistory originated in his preschool days, and has continued to grow with his increasing involvement in this field.

His concern for the rapidly vanishing culture of the once extensive Carnarvon tribes became a fulltime commitment several years ago when he joined the Queensland National Parks and Wildlife Service. His work as Aboriginal art site recorder has permitted him to continue his research into the area's prehistory. In *The Roof of Queensland* (University of Queensland Press, 1983) he wrote and photographed a captivating tribute to his beloved Carnarvon Gorge.

With the recent increase in the numbers of visitors to the Carnarvon area national parks, it was decided to attempt to increase awareness among visitors of the significant association between the Aboriginal culture and these beautiful parks.

Working with John Morrison, a local artist and a friend of long standing, Grahame decided to prepare a series of children's books, using Aboriginal legends associated with the Carnarvons.

John Morrison (artist)

For more than twenty years John Morrison has been fascinated with the Carnarvon Ranges, and he now lives and works there for six months every year.

In association with his neighbour Grahame Walsh, John has acquired an interest in the archaeology of Aboriginal prehistory in the Carnarvon area.

John's painting includes oils and acrylics, however for the colour illustrations in this book he turned to his specialty, watercolours.